Thank you
for a
wonderful
year!

Made in the USA
Las Vegas, NV
04 May 2021

22456245R00063